This book
belongs to:

Busy, Busy Santa Claus

Coloring Book

Mary Lou Brown & Sandy Mahony

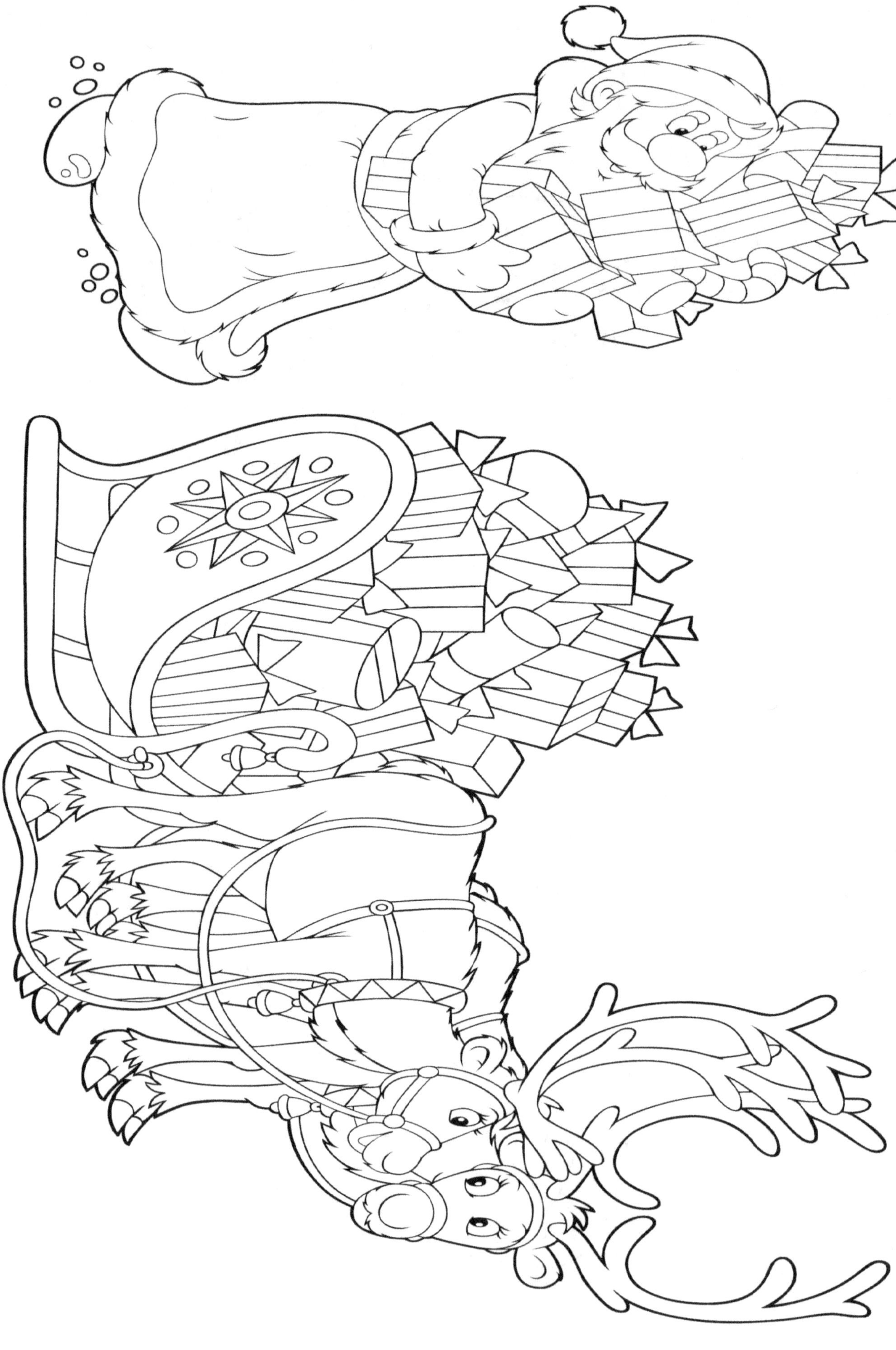

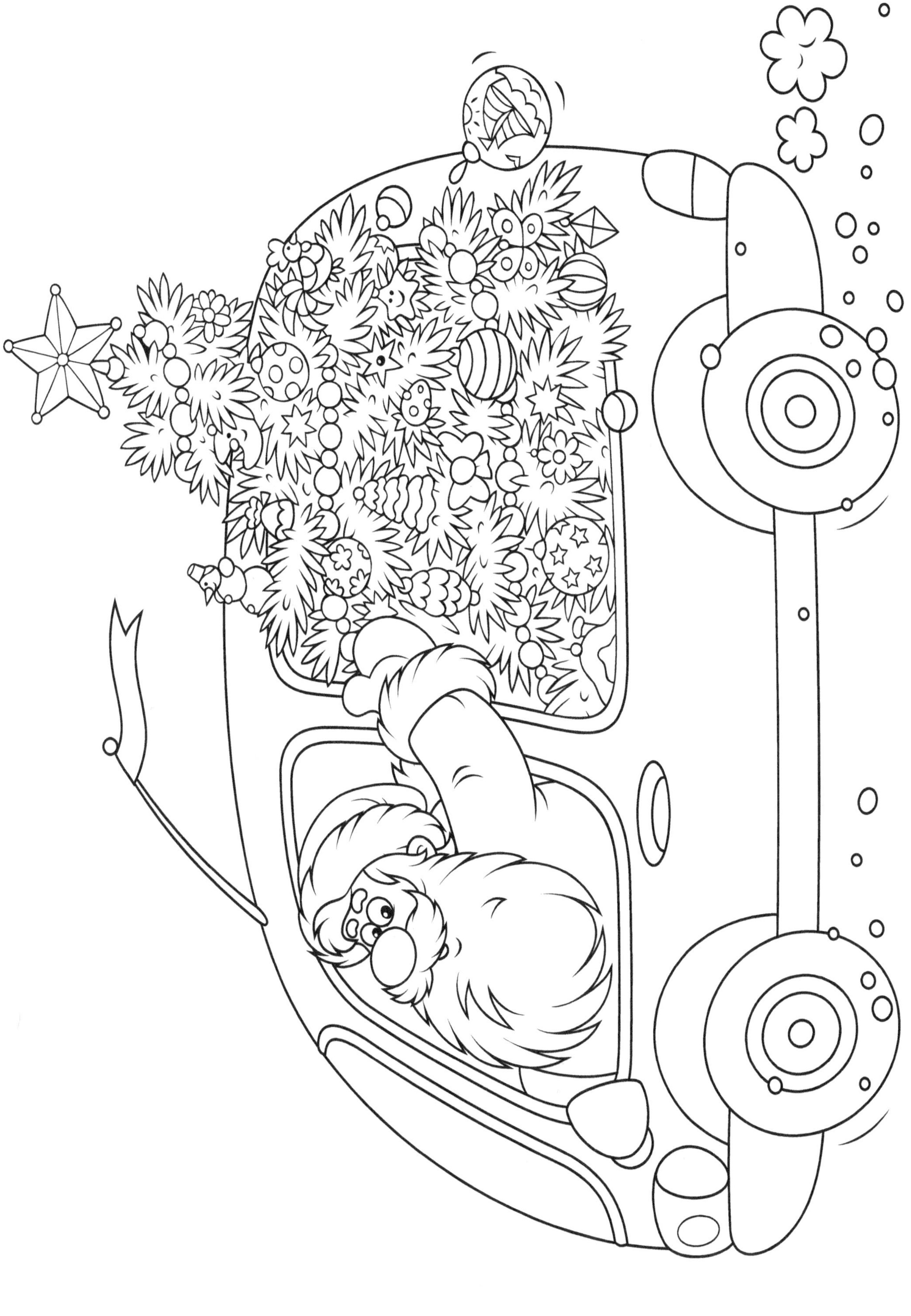

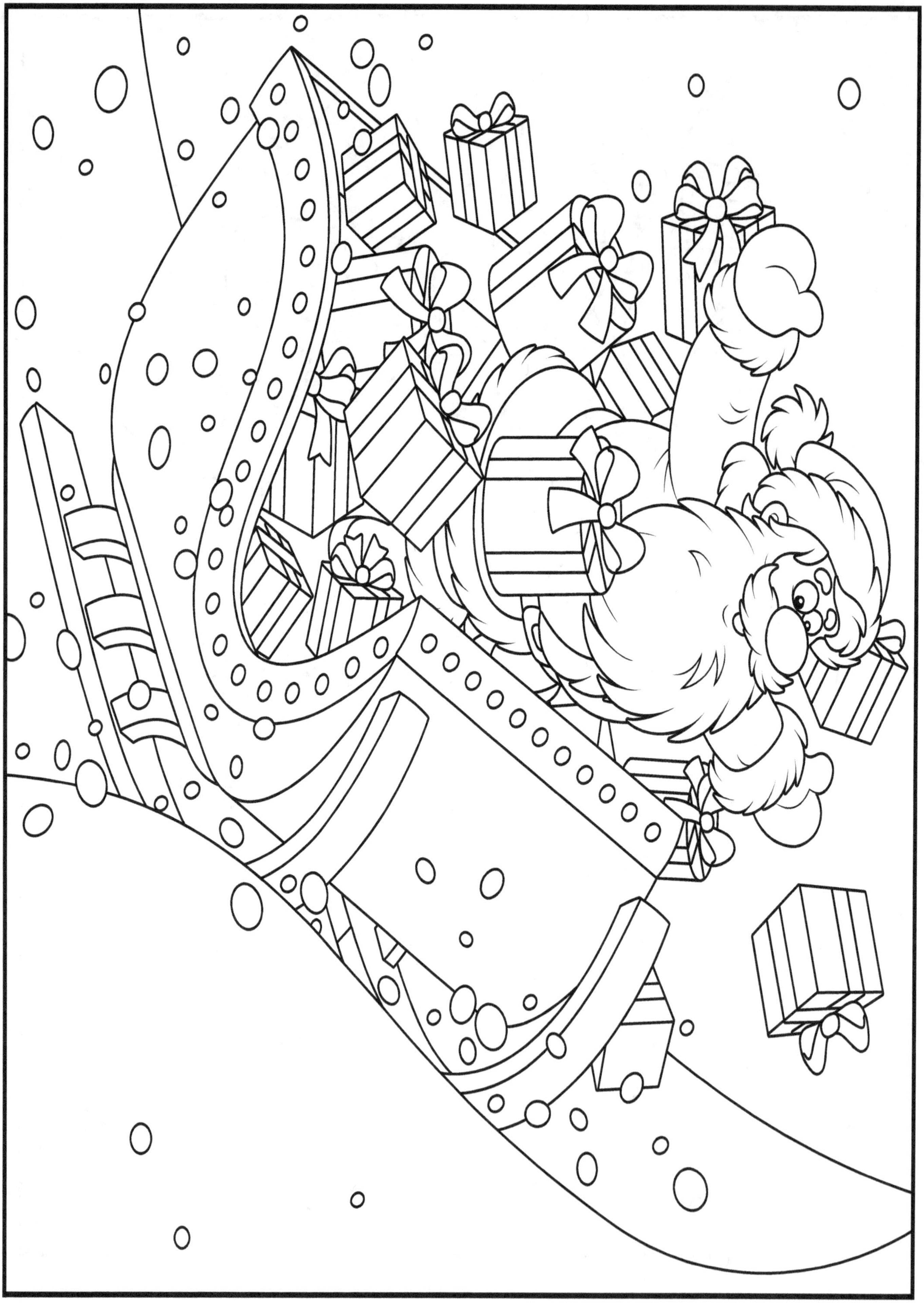

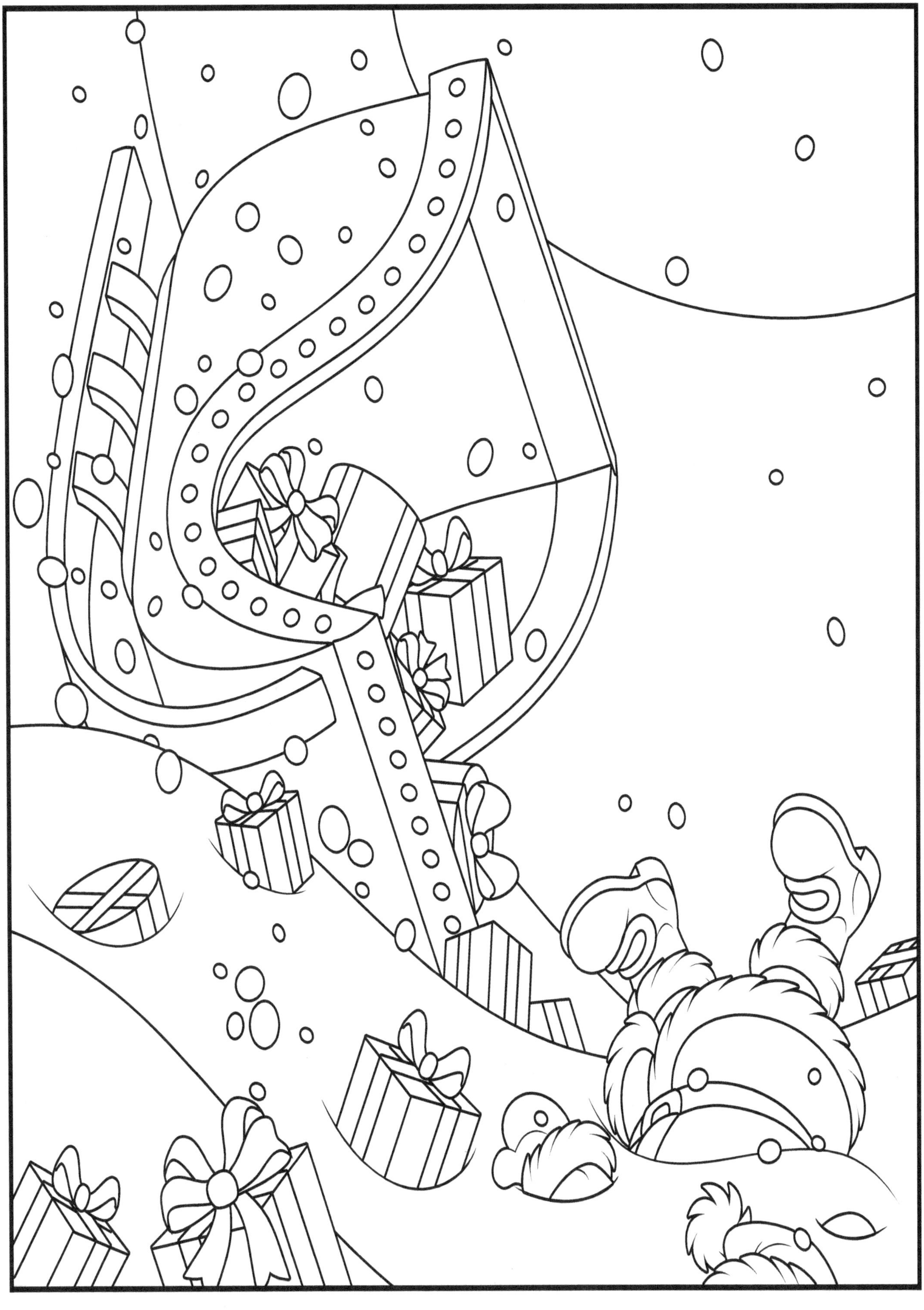

12
9
3
6

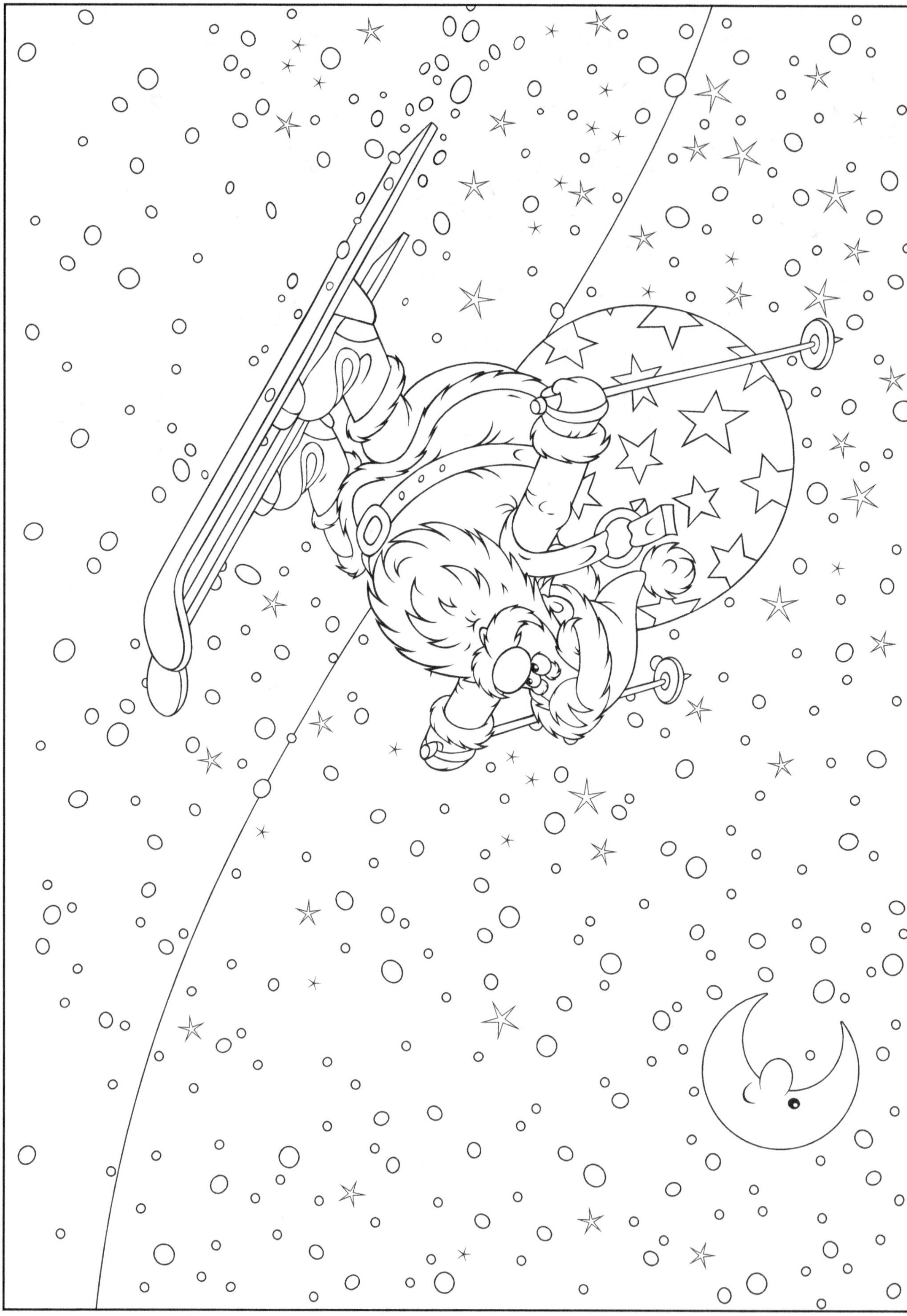

www.ingramcontent.com/pod-product-compliance
Lightning Source LLC
Chambersburg PA
CBHW081128280526
45787CB00007B/3015
* 9 7 8 1 5 3 5 0 0 7 2 8 3 *